Descendants of Benjamin Franklin Simmons

Generation 1

1. **BENJAMIN FRANKLIN**[1] **SIMMONS** was born in Jan 1872 in Georgia. He died between 08 Jan 1920-14 Apr 1930. He married Nancy Ann Johnson, daughter of Thomas H. Johnson and Courtney Jones about 1897. She was born on 11 Feb 1873 in Dooley County, Georgia. She died on 13 Feb 1966 in Appling County, Georgia.

More About Benjamin Franklin Simmons:
Living In: 1900 Rabbitville, Clinch County, Georgia
Living In: 1910 Graham, Appling County, Georgia
Living In: 1920 Surrency, Appling County, Georgia
Occupation: Farmer

More About Nancy Ann Johnson:
Burial: Ten Mile Creek Baptist Church Cemetery, Appling County, Georgia
Living In: 1930 As a widow in Deems, Appling County, Georgia

Notes for Nancy Ann Johnson:
Birth and death dates are from Ten Mile Creek Baptist Church Cemetery. Georgia death index gives birth year as 1873 and date of death as February 13, 1966.

Benjamin Franklin Simmons and Nancy Ann Johnson had the following children:

    i.   MAUDE BETHEL[2] SIMMONS was born on 22 Feb 1899 in Georgia. She married Forest S. Sapp on 30 May 1929 in Appling County, Georgia. He was born about 1909 in Georgia.

    ii.   HARVEY WESLEY SIMMONS was born on 22 Sep 1902 in Georgia.

3.   iii.   BERTIE EVELYN SIMMONS was born on 27 Sep 1904 in Appling County, Georgia. She died on 20 Nov 1934 in Deens, Appling County, Georgia. She married John James Crews on 22 Mar 1926 in Appling County, Georgia. He was born on 26 Sep 1906 in Baker County, Florida. He died on 14 Dec 1963 in Charlton County, Georgia.

    iv.   BEULAH VICTORIA SIMMONS was born on 15 Jan 1906 in Georgia. She died on 26 Nov 1973 in Georgia. She married C. M. Turner on 19 Aug 1933 in Appling County, Georgia.

More About Beulah Victoria Simmons:
Burial: Ten Mile Creek Baptist Church Cemetery, Appling County, Georgia

    v.   JESSIE GERTRUDE SIMMONS was born on 27 Jan 1907 in Baxley, Appling County, Georgia. She died on 20 Oct 1970 in Brunswick, Georgia. She married ROBERT TURNER.

    vi.   RILLA ROSSETER SIMMONS was born on 12 Sep 1909 in Appling County, Georgia. She died on 13 Jan 1988 in Brunswick, Georgia. She married John Lewis Godley on 03 Jul 1938 in Camden, Georgia. He was born on 05 Dec 1907 in Camden, Georgia. He died on 17 May 2003 in Brunswick, Georgia.

More About Rilla Rosseter Simmons:
Burial: Palmetto Cemetery, Brunswick, Georgia

vii.   FRANCES MAE SIMMONS was born about 1911 in Georgia.

3.   viii. EDWARD SIMMONS was born about 1912 in Georgia. He married MONTEEN TURNER. She was born on 28 Feb 1916 in Hall County, Georgia. She died on 16 Jun 1984 in Brunswick, Georgia.

ix.   WILLIS C. SIMMONS was born about 1915 in Georgia.

x.   BENJAMIN F. SIMMONS was born about Jun 1916 in Georgia. He died in 1934.

xi.   ELIZABETH V. SIMMONS was born about Apr 1919 in Georgia.

Generation 2

2.   **BERTIE EVELYN^2 SIMMONS** (Benjamin Franklin^1) was born on 27 Sep 1904 in Appling County, Georgia. She died on 20 Nov 1934 in Deens, Appling County, Georgia. She married John James Crews on 22 Mar 1926 in Appling County, Georgia. He was born on 26 Sep 1906 in Baker County, Florida. He died on 14 Dec 1963 in Charlton County, Georgia.

John James Crews and Bertie Evelyn Simmons had the following child:

i.   JAMES THOMAS^3 CREWS was born on 18 Feb 1929 in Appling County, Georgia. He died on 16 Jan 1984 in Columbia County, Florida.

3.   **EDWARD^2 SIMMONS** (Benjamin Franklin^1) was born about 1912 in Georgia. He married **MONTEEN TURNER**. She was born on 28 Feb 1916 in Hall County, Georgia. She died on 16 Jun 1984 in Brunswick, Georgia.

More About Edward Simmons:
Living In: 1920 Surrency, Georgia
Living In: 1930 Deems, Georgia

More About Monteen Turner:
Burial: 19 Jun 1984 in Pleasant Grove Cemetery, Baxley, Georgia
Living In: 1984 Sterling Community, Glynn County, Georgia
Occupation: Worked thirty years for SeaPak Shrimp Company on St. Simons Island, Glynn County, Georgia

Notes for Monteen Turner:
SIMMONS, Monteen (Turner)
The Brunswick News; Monday 18 June 1984; pg. 3A col. 5

SIMMONS FUNERAL BEING HELD TODAY
Services for Monteen Turner Simmons, 68, a resident of Sterling who died early Saturday at the Glynn-Brunswick Memorial Hospital after a short illness will be held Tuesday.
She was a native of Appling County and had been a resident of Glynn County for the past 35 years. She had been employed by Sea-Pak for the past 30 years. She was a member of the Holiness Church in Baxley.
She is survived by two daughters, Willene Lott of St. Simons and Lulene Tison of Sterling. Two sons, Edward W. Simmons of Plant City, Fla. and Gary Simmons of Sterling; two sisters, Irene Carter of Baxley and Pauline Sellers of Savannah; a brother Bill Turner of Baxley; seven grandchildren; two great-grandchildren; several nieces and nephews.
Services will be held Tuesday at 1 p.m. in the chapel of Edo Miller & Sons Funeral with the Rev. Dorris Black officiating. Entombment services will be held at 3:30 p.m. in Pleasant Grove Cemetery near Baxley.

The family will receive friends at the funeral home tonight from 6 until 9 o'clock. Edo Miller & Sons Funeral Home is in charge of arrangements.

Edward Simmons and Monteen Turner had the following children:

4.   i.   EDWARD WILTON[3] SIMMONS was born on 29 Aug 1935 in Georgia. He died on 23 Apr 1997 in Hillsborough County, Florida. He married LEONA RYALS. She was born on 14 Aug 1939 in Georgia.

5.   ii.   WILLEEN SIMMONS. She married ARCHIE LOTT.

6.   iii.   LULLEEN SIMMONS. She married BUTCH TISON.

      iv.   GARY SIMMONS was born in Glynn County, Georgia.

      v.   INFANT DAUGHTER SIMMONS was born on 14 Jul 1956 in Glynn County, Georgia. She died on 14 Jul 1956.

Notes for Infant Daughter Simmons:
Lived for ten minutes.

Generation 3

4.   EDWARD WILTON[3] SIMMONS (Edward[2], Benjamin Franklin[1]) was born on 29 Aug 1935 in Georgia. He died on 23 Apr 1997 in Hillsborough County, Florida. He married LEONA RYALS. She was born on 14 Aug 1939 in Georgia.

More About Edward Wilton Simmons:
Burial: Hopewell Memorial Gardens, Plant City, Florida

Edward Wilton Simmons and Leona Ryals had the following child:

7.   i.   MARK Edward[4] SIMMONS was born on 29 Oct 1967. He married (1) DIANA GAIL EDWARDS on 23 Dec 1988 in Plant City, Florida. She was born on 28 Mar 1969 in Plant City, Florida. He married SHERRI (UNKNOWN). He married NANCY SANTIAGO CLARIDY.

5.   WILLEEN[3] SIMMONS (Edward[2], Benjamin Franklin[1]). She married ARCHIE LOTT.

Archie Lott and Willeen Simmons had the following child:

      i.   RICHIE[4] LOTT.

6.   LULLEEN[3] SIMMONS (Edward[2], Benjamin Franklin[1]). She married BUTCH TISON.

Butch Tison and Lulleen Simmons had the following child:

      i.   ANN[4] TISON.

Generation 4

7.   MARK Edward[4] SIMMONS (Edward Wilton[3], Edward[2], Benjamin Franklin[1]) was born on 29 Oct 1967. He married (1) DIANA GAIL EDWARDS on 23 Dec 1988 in Plant City, Florida. She was born on 28 Mar 1969 in Plant City, Florida. He married SHERRI (UNKNOWN). He married NANCY SANTIAGO

CLARIDY.

Mark Edward Simmons and Diana Gail Edwards had the following children:

8.   i. MARK GREGORY[5] EDWARDS was born on 20 Jun 1988 in Plant City, Florida. He married Julie Ann Mercer on 17 Feb 2007 in Wellston, Ohio. She was born on 28 May 1988.

9.   ii. DAVIAN GAIL SIMMONS was born on 12 Feb 1991 in Monroe, North Carolina. She married Jerrod Elden Rogers, son of James J. Rogers and Betty Lou Eberts on 24 Mar 2012 in Berlin Crossroads, Jackson County, Ohio. He was born on 17 Mar 1987 in Ohio.

Mark Edward Simmons and Sherri (unknown) had the following child:

10.   iii. MARISSA DAWN (UNKNOWN) was born on 11 Aug 1987. She married JARED REEVES. He was born on 28 Feb 1988.

Mark Edward Simmons and Nancy Santiago Claridy had the following child:

11.   iv. ASHLEY NICOLE SIMMONS was born on 21 Oct 1985. She married JUSTIN HELMS. He was born on 26 Jan 1986.

Generation 5

8.   MARK GREGORY[5] EDWARDS (Mark Edward[4] Simmons, Edward Wilton[3] Simmons, Edward[2] Simmons, Benjamin Franklin[1] Simmons) was born on 20 Jun 1988 in Plant City, Florida. He married Julie Ann Mercer on 17 Feb 2007 in Wellston, Ohio. She was born on 28 May 1988.

Mark Gregory Edwards and Julie Ann Mercer had the following children:

    i.   SOPHIA MARIE[6] EDWARDS was born on 05 Aug 2010 in Chillicothe, Ohio.

    ii.   MARK WILTON EDWARDS was born on 28 Oct 2013 in Columbus, Ohio.

9.   DAVIAN GAIL[5] SIMMONS (Mark Edward[4], Edward Wilton[3], Edward[2], Benjamin Franklin[1]) was born on 12 Feb 1991 in Monroe, North Carolina. She married Jerrod Elden Rogers, son of James J. Rogers and Betty Lou Eberts on 24 Mar 2012 in Berlin Crossroads, Jackson County, Ohio. He was born on 17 Mar 1987 in Ohio.

Jerrod Elden Rogers and Davian Gail Simmons had the following children:

    i.   DAVID[6] ROGERS was born on 03 May 2014 in Athens, Ohio.

    ii.   CLOE GAIL ROGERS was born on 14 May 2016 in Athens, Ohio.

10.   MARISSA DAWN[5] (UNKNOWN) (Mark Edward[4] Simmons, Edward Wilton[3] Simmons, Edward[2] Simmons, Benjamin Franklin[1] Simmons) was born on 11 Aug 1987. She married JARED REEVES. He was born on 28 Feb 1988.

Jared Reeves and Marissa Dawn (unknown) had the following child:

    i.   COLTON[6] REEVES was born on 18 Oct 2013.

11.   ASHLEY NICOLE[5] SIMMONS (Mark Edward[4], Edward Wilton[3], Edward[2], Benjamin Franklin[1]) was born on 21 Oct 1985. She married JUSTIN HELMS. He was born on 26 Jan 1986.

Justin Helms and Ashley Nicole Simmons had the following children:

    i.   AUDRA DENISE[6] HELMS was born on 02 Nov 2009.

ii. JUSTIN LEVI HELMS was born on 15 Mar 2015.

Notes:

Descendants of Micajah Turner

Generation 1

1. **MICAJAH[1] TURNER** was born in 1777 in Virginia. He died on 01 Nov 1871 in Cleveland, White County, Georgia. He married Nancy (unknown) in 1795 in Virginia. She was born in 1777 in Virginia. She died about 1875 in White County, Georgia.

More About Micajah Turner:
Burial: Tesnatee Baptist Church Cemetery, Cleveland, White County, Georgia
Living In: 1850 Habersham County, Georgia
Living In:1860 White County, Georgia
Living In: 1870 White County, Georgia

Notes for Micajah Turner:
Date of death is from headstone at Tesnatee Baptist Church Cemetery.

More About Nancy (unknown):
Burial: Tesnatee Baptist Church Cemetery, Cleveland, White County, Georgia

Micajah Turner and Nancy (unknown) had the following children:

    1.   JOSEPH[2] TURNER was born about 1796 in South Carolina.

    2.   JOHN BERRYMAN TURNER was born on 01 May 1798 in South Carolina.

2.   iii. HENRY TURNER was born about 1800 in South Carolina. He married CELIA (UNKNOWN). She was born about 1806 in North Carolina.

    iv.   SUSANNAH TURNER was born about 1802 in South Carolina.

    v.   WILLIAM TURNER was born about 1805 in South Carolina.

3.   vi. JARRETT TURNER was born on 06 May 1806 in South Carolina. He died on 03 Jan 1857 in Union County, Georgia. He married Sarah Collins, daughter of Thompson Collins and Celia (unknown) on 19 Jul 1830 in Habersham County, Georgia. She was born on 16 Feb 1812 in Buncombe County, North Carolina. She died on 16 Jan 1867.

    vii.   JESSE TURNER was born about 1808 in South Carolina.

    viii.   SABRAY TURNER was born about 1810 in South Carolina.

    ix.   HIRAM TURNER was born about 1811 in South Carolina.

    x.   BUTLER TURNER was born between 1815-1820 in Habersham County, Georgia.

    xi.   NANCY TURNER was born on 16 Jul 1825 in Habersham County, Georgia.

    xii.   MICAJAH TURNER was born in 1830 in Habersham County, Georgia.

Generation 2

2. **HENRY[2] TURNER** (Micajah[1]) was born about 1800 in South Carolina. He married **CELIA (UNKNOWN)**. She was born about 1806 in North Carolina.

More About Henry Turner:
Living In: 1850 Habersham County, Georgia
Living In: Bet. 1860-1880 White County, Georgia

Notes for Henry Turner:
Living next door to his parents in 1870.

Henry Turner and Celia (unknown) had the following children:

    i.   BERRY H.[3] TURNER was born about 1845 in Georgia.

    ii.   HIRAM TURNER was born about 1848 in Georgia.

    iii.   JAMES TURNER was born about 1849 in Georgia.

    iv.   MELINDA TURNER was born about 1846 in Georgia.

    v.   REBECCA TURNER was born about 1848 in Georgia.

    vi.   JESSE TURNER was born about 1852 in Georgia.

3.   JARRETT[2] TURNER (Micajah[1]) was born on 06 May 1806 in South Carolina. He died on 03 Jan 1857 in Union County, Georgia. He married Sarah Collins, daughter of Thompson Collins and Celia (unknown) on 19 Jul 1830 in Habersham County, Georgia. She was born on 16 Feb 1812 in Buncombe County, North Carolina. She died on 16 Jan 1867.

More About Jarrett Turner:
Living In: 1850 Union County, Georgia

More About Sarah Collins:
Living In: 1860 Union County, Georgia

Jarrett Turner and Sarah Collins had the following children:

    i.   CELIA[3] TURNER was born on 25 Dec 1831 in Habersham County, Georgia.

    ii.   NANCY TURNER was born on 29 Nov 1832 in Union County, Georgia.

    iii.   FRANCIS MARION TURNER was born on 24 Aug 1834 in Union County, Georgia.

    iv.   ELIZABETH TURNER was born on 17 Jan 1836 in Union County, Georgia.

    v.   RUTH TURNER was born on 10 Dec 1837 in Union County, Georgia.

5.   vi. JAMES JARRETT TURNER was born on 25 Jul 1840 in Habersham County, Georgia. He died on 30 Sep 1899 in Hall County, Georgia. He married Mary Elizabeth Dyer, daughter of Micajah Dyer and Harriet Hall on 28 Mar 1858 in Union County, Georgia. She was born in 1842 in Union County, Georgia. She died on 10 Nov 1910.

    vii.   SARAH CAROLINE TURNER was born on 17 Jun 1842 in Union County, Georgia.

8. PHOEBE TURNER was born on 16 Oct 1844 in Union County, Georgia.

9. MICAJAH TURNER was born on 03 Aug 1847 in Union County, Georgia.

10. OLIVE S. TURNER was born on 30 Sep 1849 in Union County, Georgia.

11. WILLIAM PRUITT TURNER was born on 21 Apr 1852 in Union County, Georgia.

12. THOMPSON TURNER was born on 29 Jul 1854 in Union County, Georgia.

Generation 3

4. JAMES JARRETT[3] TURNER (Jarrett[2], Micajah[1]) was born on 25 Jul 1840 in Habersham County, Georgia. He died on 30 Sep 1899 in Hall County, Georgia. He married Mary Elizabeth Dyer, daughter of Micajah Dyer and Harriet Hall on 28 Mar 1858 in Union County, Georgia. She was born in 1842 in Union County, Georgia. She died on 10 Nov 1910.

More About James Jarrett Turner:
Living In: 1860 Union County, Georgia
Living In: 1870 Union County, Georgia
Living In: 1880 Naramore, Hall County, Georgia
Occupation: 1880; Running Grist Mill
Occupation: 1860 and 1870, Farmer

James Jarrett Turner and Mary Elizabeth Dyer had the following children:

i. MICAJAH LUMPKIN[4] TURNER was born on 26 Feb 1859 in Union County, Georgia.

6. ii. WILLIAM FRANKLIN TURNER was born on 03 Jul 1861 in Union County, Georgia. He died on 20 Aug 1919 in Banks County, Georgia. He married VADA PAYNE. She was born in Mar 1869 in Georgia. He married CORA LEE CANUP. She was born on 24 Dec 1890 in Hall County, Georgia. She died on 22 Aug 1980 in Baxley, Georgia.

Generation 4

5. WILLIAM FRANKLIN[4] TURNER (James Jarrett[3], Jarrett[2], Micajah[1]) was born on 03 Jul 1861 in Union County, Georgia. He died on 20 Aug 1919 in Banks County, Georgia. He married VADA PAYNE. She was born in Mar 1869 in Georgia. He married CORA LEE CANUP. She was born on 24 Dec 1890 in Hall County, Georgia. She died on 22 Aug 1980 in Baxley, Georgia.

More About William Franklin Turner:
Living In: 1900 Polksville District, Hall County, Georgia
Occupation: Farmer

William Franklin Turner and Vada Payne had the following children:

i. ETTA MAE[5] TURNER was born in Dec 1884 in Georgia.

ii. JAMES ANDREW TURNER was born in Jun 1887 in Georgia. He died on 09 Mar 1948 in Baldwin County, Georgia. He married VIOLA JESSE BUFFINGTON. She was born on 31 Aug 1886 in Hall County, Georgia. She died on 26 Jul 1978 in Hall County, Georgia.

More About James Andrew Turner:
Living In: 1948 Hall County, Georgia

Occupation: 1900; Farm Labor

iii.   JOSEPH TURNER was born in Apr 1889 in Georgia.

More About Joseph Turner:
Occupation: 1900; Farm Labor

iv.   CLAUDE LIVINGSTON TURNER was born on 05 Jun 1891 in Georgia. He died on 30 Sep 1962 in Baldwin County, Georgia. He married RADER DODD. She was born on 07 Nov 1897. She died on 26 Jan 1964 in Hall County, Georgia.

More About Claude Livingston Turner:
Burial: Bellton Baptist Church Cemetery, Hall County, Georgia
Living In: Sep 1962 Hall County, Georgia

v.   WALTER TURNER was born in Apr 1894 in Georgia.

6.   vi. ALBERT OLIVER TURNER was born on 03 Feb 1897 in Hall County, Georgia. He died on 29 Sep 1976 in Chatham County, Georgia. He married Lousiana Canup, daughter of Newton James Canup and Nancy Amanda Jenkins in Hall County, Georgia. She was born on 19 Aug 1896 in Hall County, Georgia. She died on 25 Apr 1965 in Baxley, Georgia.

vii.   SALLIE TURNER was born in Sep 1899 in Georgia.

More About Cora Lee Canup:
Burial: 24 Aug 1980 in Ten Mile Creek Baptist Church Cemetery, Baxley, Appling County, Georgia
Living In: 1920 Cora and her children are living with her parents in Narramore District, Hall County, Georgia

William Franklin Turner and Cora Lee Canup had the following children:

viii.   ROBERT NEWTON TURNER was born on 21 Apr 1909 in Hall County, Georgia. He died on 27 Mar 1980 in Baxley, Georgia. He married Maybell C. Carter, daughter of Chatman Carter and Lula Sapp on 29 Oct 1929. She was born on 28 May 1911. She died on 26 Jan 1996 in Appling County, Georgia.

ix.   MAMIE L. TURNER was born on 17 Nov 1910 in Banks County, Georgia. She died on 6 Jan 1998 in Baxley, Georgia. She married LLOYD G. STEEDLEY. He was born on 27 Jul 1898 in Appling County, Georgia. He died on 22 Dec 1956 in Appling County, Georgia.

More About Mamie L. Turner:
Burial: Appling County, Georgia

x.   MAGGIE BEATRICE TURNER was born on 26 Nov 1912 in Banks County, Georgia. She died on 10 Mar 1983 in Glynn County, Georgia. She married CLARENCE EARVIN CHASTEEN. He was born in Appling County, Georgia. He died on 16 Dec 1965 in Glynn County, Georgia.

More About Maggie Beatrice Turner:
Burial: Appling County, Georgia

xi.   ELDORA TURNER was born about 1914 in Banks County, Georgia. She died about 1926 in Hall County, Georgia.

7.   xii.   MOENA LEVADA TURNER was born on 27 Apr 1917 in Banks County, Georgia. She married HERMAN JAMES COBIA. He was born on 11 Feb 1919 in Eastman, Georgia. He died on 05 May 1970 in Gulfport, Mississippi.

xiii.   JOHN HENRY TURNER was born on 01 Feb 1920 in Hall County, Georgia. He died on 12 Oct 2002 in Appling County, Georgia. He married BEATRICE WEAVER. He married VERDIE MAE HUGHES. She was born in 1938 in Georgia. She died in 1955 in Appling County, Georgia.

More About John Henry Turner:
Burial: Appling County, Georgia
Burial: Old Pleasant Grove Cemetery, Baxley, Georgia

Generation 5

6.   **ALBERT OLIVER[5] TURNER** (William Franklin[4], James Jarrett[3], Jarrett[2], Micajah[1]) was born on 03 Feb 1897 in Hall County, Georgia. He died on 29 Sep 1976 in Chatham County, Georgia. He married Lousiana Canup, daughter of Newton James Canup and Nancy Amanda Jenkins in Hall County, Georgia. She was born on 19 Aug 1896 in Hall County, Georgia. She died on 25 Apr 1965 in Baxley, Georgia.

More About Albert Oliver Turner:
Burial: Old Pleasant Grove Cemetery, Appling County, Georgia
Living In: 1900 Polksville District, Hall County, Georgia
Living In: 1920 Narramore District, Hall County, Georgia
Living In: 1930 Appling County, Georgia
Living In:1976 Baxley, Georgia
Occupation: Farmer

Notes for Albert Oliver Turner:
World War One draft registration gives birth date as February 3, 1897. Headstone gives birth date as January 3, 1899. Birth date in 1900 Federal census is January 1897. Social security death index gives birthdate as January 3, 1899.

More About Lousiana Canup:
Burial: 27 Apr 1965 in Old Pleasant Grove Cemetery, Appling County, Georgia
Occupation: 1920; Works on horse farm

Notes for Lousiana Canup:
Used Lucy instead of Lousiana for given name.
Family members remember her maiden name as Canup. Funeral home records show her parents as Amanda Jenkins and Tom Bryant.

Albert Oliver Turner and Lousiana Canup had the following children:

8.   i.   MONTEEN[6] TURNER was born on 28 Feb 1916 in Hall County, Georgia. She died on 16 Jun 1984 in Brunswick, Georgia. She married EDWARD SIMMONS. He was born about 1912 in Georgia.

9.   ii.   TALMADGE TURNER was born on 27 Sep 1917 in Hall County, Georgia. He died on

16 Aug 1983 in Baxley, Georgia. He married Inez Altman on 08 Jan 1945 in Appling County, Georgia. She was born on 02 Oct 1928 in Georgia. She died on 01 Jul 2007 in Baxley, Georgia.

10. iii. IRENE TURNER was born on 30 Jun 1922 in Hall County, Georgia. She died on 07 Aug 1988 in Appling County, Georgia. She married James B. Carter, son of James Carter and Allie Sapp on 06 Jun 1942 in Appling County, Georgia. He was born on 29 Mar 1924 in Appling County, Georgia. He died on 29 Jul 2003 in Appling County, Georgia.

11. iv. WILLIAM THOMAS TURNER was born on 10 Nov 1925 in Hall County, Georgia. He died on 05 Aug 2004 in Appling County, Georgia. He married Eleanor Lightsey, daughter of Kenneth Lightsey and Myrtle Tyre in Appling County, Georgia. She was born on 06 Jul 1931 in Appling County, Georgia. She died on 18 Feb 1994 in Appling County, Georgia.

12. v. PAULINE TURNER was born on 10 Nov 1928 in Appling County, Georgia. She died on 29 Oct 2002 in Appling County, Georgia. She married DWIGHT SELLERS. He was born in Appling County, Georgia.

 vii. INFANT DAUGHTER TURNER.

7. **MOENA LEVADA^5 TURNER** (William Franklin^4, James Jarrett^3, Jarrett^2, Micajah^1) was born on 27 Apr 1917 in Banks County, Georgia. She married **HERMAN JAMES COBIA**. He was born on 11 Feb 1919 in Eastman, Georgia. He died on 05 May 1970 in Gulfport, Mississippi.

More About Herman James Cobia:

Burial: Harrison County, Mississippi

Herman James Cobia and Moena Levada Turner had the following child:

 i. ELLA MYRTICE^6 COBIA was born on 12 Nov 1940 in Baxley, Georgia.

Generation 6

8. **MONTEEN^6 TURNER** (Albert Oliver^5, William Franklin^4, James Jarrett^3, Jarrett^2, Micajah^1) was born on 28 Feb 1916 in Hall County, Georgia. She died on 16 Jun 1984 in Brunswick, Georgia. She married **EDWARD SIMMONS**. He was born about 1912 in Georgia.

More About Monteen Turner:
Burial: 19 Jun 1984 in Pleasant Grove Cemetery, Baxley, Georgia
Living In: 1984 Sterling Community, Glynn County, Georgia
Occupation: Worked thirty years for SeaPak Shrimp Company on St. Simons Island, Glynn County, Georgia

Notes for Monteen Turner:
SIMMONS, Monteen (Turner)
The Brunswick News; Monday 18 June 1984; pg. 3A col. 5

SIMMONS FUNERAL BEING HELD TODAY
Services for Monteen Turner Simmons, 68, a resident of Sterling who died early Saturday at the Glynn-Brunswick Memorial Hospital after a short illness will be held Tuesday.
She was a native of Appling County and had been a resident of Glynn County for the past 35 years. She had been employed by Sea-Pak for the past 30 years. She was a member of the Holiness Church in Baxley.

She is survived by two daughters, Willene Lott of St. Simons and Lulene Tison of Sterling. Two sons, Edward W. Simmons of Plant City, Fla. and Gary Simmons of Sterling; two sisters, Irene Carter of Baxley and Pauline Sellers of Savannah; a brother Bill Turner of Baxley; seven grandchildren; two great-grandchildren; several nieces and nephews.
Services will be held Tuesday at 1 p.m. in the chapel of Edo Miller & Sons Funeral with the Rev. Dorris Black officiating. Entombment services will be held at 3:30 p.m. in Pleasant Grove Cemetery near Baxley.
The family will receive friends at the funeral home tonight from 6 until 9 o'clock. Edo Miller & Sons Funeral Home is in charge of arrangements.

More About Edward Simmons:
Living In: 1920 Surrency, Georgia
Living In: 1930 Deems, Georgia

Edward Simmons and Monteen Turner had the following children:

13.	i. EDWARD WILTON[7] SIMMONS was born on 29 Aug 1935 in Georgia. He died on 23 Apr 1997 in Hillsborough County, Florida. He married LEONA RYALS. She was born on 14 Aug 1939 in Georgia.

14.	ii. WILLEEN SIMMONS. She married ARCHIE LOTT.

15.	iii. LULLEEN SIMMONS. She married BUTCH TISON.

	iv. GARY SIMMONS was born in Glynn County, Georgia.

	v. INFANT DAUGHTER SIMMONS was born on 14 Jul 1956 in Glynn County, Georgia. She died on 14 Jul 1956.

		Notes for Infant Daughter Simmons: Lived for ten minutes.

9.	TALMADGE[6] TURNER (Albert Oliver[5], William Franklin[4], James Jarrett[3], Jarrett[2], Micajah[1]) was born on 27 Sep 1917 in Hall County, Georgia. He died on 16 Aug 1983 in Baxley, Georgia. He married Inez Altman on 08 Jan 1945 in Appling County, Georgia. She was born on 02 Oct 1928 in Georgia. She died on 01 Jul 2007 in Baxley, Georgia.

More About Talmadge Turner:
Burial: Old Pleasant Grove Cemetery, Appling County, Georgia

More About Inez Altman:
Burial: Old Pleasant Grove Cemetery, Appling County, Georgia

Talmadge Turner and Inez Altman had the following child:

16.	i. BILLY[7] TURNER was born on 28 Mar 1946 in Appling County, Georgia. He married Virginia (unknown) in Appling County, Georgia.

10.	IRENE[6] TURNER (Albert Oliver[5], William Franklin[4], James Jarrett[3], Jarrett[2], Micajah[1]) was born on 30 Jun 1922 in Hall County, Georgia. She died on 07 Aug 1988 in Appling County, Georgia. She married James B. Carter, son of James Carter and Allie Sapp on 06 Jun 1942 in Appling County, Georgia. He was born on 29 Mar 1924 in Appling County, Georgia. He died on 29 Jul 2003 in

Appling County, Georgia.

More About Irene Turner:
Burial: Appling County, Georgia

More About James B. Carter:
Burial: 31 Jul 2003 in Appling County, Georgia
Occupation: Sheriff of Appling County, Georgia August 1960-1976
Occupation: Chief of Police, Baxley, Georgia, 1976-1979
Military Service: U.S. Army, World War Two

James B. Carter and Irene Turner had the following children:

17. i. ELAINE[7] CARTER was born on 17 Nov 1943. She married (1) RICHARD EASON in Appling County, Georgia. He was born in Appling County, Georgia. She married RONNIE DOWDNEY. He was born on 22 Nov 1946.

18. ii. EILEEN CARTER was born on 21 Sep 1946 in Appling County, Georgia. She died on 15 Sep 2010 in Appling County, Georgia. She married (1) JOE VESTON LIGHTSEY, son of George Lightsey and Senia Pearce in Nov 1963. He was born on 05 Mar 1944 in Appling County, Georgia. She married WAYNE HARRIS.

11. **WILLIAM THOMAS[6] TURNER** (Albert Oliver[5], William Franklin[4], James Jarrett[3], Jarrett[2], Micajah[1]) was born on 10 Nov 1925 in Hall County, Georgia. He died on 05 Aug 2004 in Appling County, Georgia. He married Eleanor Lightsey, daughter of Kenneth Lightsey and Myrtle Tyre in Appling County, Georgia. She was born on 06 Jul 1931 in Appling County, Georgia. She died on 18 Feb 1994 in Appling County, Georgia.

More About William Thomas Turner:
Burial: 06 Aug 2004 in Pine Grove Freewill Baptist Church, Appling County, Georgia

More About Eleanor Lightsey:
Burial: Pine Grove Freewill Baptist Church, Appling County, Georgia

William Thomas Turner and Eleanor Lightsey had the following children:

 i. JOAN[7] TURNER was born on 06 Aug 1949 in Appling County, Georgia. She died on 18 Feb 1951 in Appling County, Georgia.

  More About Joan Turner:
  Burial: Pine Grove Freewill Baptist Church, Appling County, Georgia

 ii. WILLIAM TERRY TURNER was born on 19 Mar 1956.

 iii. SANDY TURNER was born on 23 Jun 1974.

12. **PAULINE[6] TURNER** (Albert Oliver[5], William Franklin[4], James Jarrett[3], Jarrett[2], Micajah[1]) was born on 10 Nov 1928 in Appling County, Georgia. She died on 29 Oct 2002 in Appling County, Georgia. She married **DWIGHT SELLERS**. He was born in Appling County, Georgia.

More About Pauline Turner:
Burial: 01 Nov 2002 in Zion Baptist Church Cemetery, Appling County, Georgia

Dwight Sellers and Pauline Turner had the following children:

i. JUNE[7] SELLERS was born in 1955 in Appling County, Georgia.

19. ii. KENNETH LEE SELLERS was born on 10 Apr 1958 in Appling County, Georgia. He died on 18 Jul 2004 in Savannah, Georgia. He married KAREN KESSEL. She was born on 15 Aug 1961.

20. iii. DONNA PATRICIA SELLERS was born on 05 Mar 1965. She married JOHN HODGES. He was born on 07 Aug 1961.

Generation 7

13. **EDWARD WILTON[7] SIMMONS** (Monteen[6] Turner, Albert Oliver[5] Turner, William Franklin[4] Turner, James Jarrett[3] Turner, Jarrett[2] Turner, Micajah[1] Turner) was born on 29 Aug 1935 in Georgia. He died on 23 Apr 1997 in Hillsborough County, Florida. He married **LEONA RYALS**. She was born on 14 Aug 1939 in Georgia.

More About Edward Wilton Simmons:
Burial: Hopewell Memorial Gardens, Plant City, Florida

Edward Wilton Simmons and Leona Ryals had the following child:
21. i. MARK EDWARD[8] SIMMONS was born on 29 Oct 1967. He married (1) DIANA GAIL EDWARDS on 23 Dec 1988 in Plant City, Florida. She was born on 28 Mar 1969 in Plant City, Florida. He married SHERRI (UNKNOWN). He married NANCY SANTIAGO CLARIDY.

14. **WILLEEN[7] SIMMONS** (Monteen[6] Turner, Albert Oliver[5] Turner, William Franklin[4] Turner, James Jarrett[3] Turner, Jarrett[2] Turner, Micajah[1] Turner, Edward, Benjamin Franklin). She married **ARCHIE LOTT**.

Archie Lott and Willeen Simmons had the following child:
i. RICHIE[8] LOTT.

15. **LULLEEN[7] SIMMONS** (Monteen[6] Turner, Albert Oliver[5] Turner, William Franklin[4] Turner, James Jarrett[3] Turner, Jarrett[2] Turner, Micajah[1] Turner, Edward, Benjamin Franklin). She married **BUTCH TISON**.

Butch Tison and Lulleen Simmons had the following child:
i. ANN[8] TISON.

16. **BILLY[7] TURNER** (Talmadge[6], Albert Oliver[5], William Franklin[4], James Jarrett[3], Jarrett[2], Micajah[1]) was born on 28 Mar 1946 in Appling County, Georgia. He married Virginia (unknown) in Appling County, Georgia.

Billy Turner and Virginia (unknown) had the following children:
22. i. MICHELLE[8] TURNER was born on 18 Jul 1965 in Appling County, Georgia. She married JOHN DARREN HENDERSON. He was born on 18 Nov 1965.

ii. BILLY ANTHONY TURNER was born on 26 Apr 1967 in Appling County, Georgia.

iii. STACEY LYNN TURNER was born on 06 Dec 1968 in Appling County, Georgia. She married BASIL MALOUF.

17. **ELAINE[7] CARTER** (Irene[6] Turner, Albert Oliver[5] Turner, William Franklin[4] Turner, James Jarrett[3] Turner, Jarrett[2] Turner, Micajah[1] Turner) was born on 17 Nov 1943. She married (1) **RICHARD**

EASON in Appling County, Georgia. He was born in Appling County, Georgia. She married
RONNIE DOWDNEY. He was born on 22 Nov 1946.

Richard Eason and Elaine Carter had the following child:

23. i. KENDRA LENEA[8] EASON was born on 20 Dec 1966 in Bacon County, Georgia. She died on
    29 Dec 1989 in Appling County, Georgia. She married Jeffery Johnson on 21 Sep
    1986 in Appling County, Georgia. He was born in Appling County, Georgia.

Ronnie Dowdney and Elaine Carter had the following child:

  i. BRITTANY RAE[8] DOWDNEY.

18. **EILEEN[7] CARTER** (Irene[6] Turner, Albert Oliver[5] Turner, William Franklin[4] Turner, James Jarrett[3]
Turner, Jarrett[2] Turner, Micajah[1] Turner) was born on 21 Sep 1946 in Appling County, Georgia.
She died on 15 Sep 2010 in Appling County, Georgia. She married (1) **JOE VESTON LIGHTSEY**,
son of George Lightsey and Senia Pearce in Nov 1963. He was born on 05 Mar 1944 in Appling
County, Georgia. She married **WAYNE HARRIS**.

More About Eileen Carter:
Burial: 18 Sep 2010 in Milliken cemetery, Appling County,
Georgia
Occupation: Shipping Supervisor

Joe Veston Lightsey and Eileen Carter had the following children:

24. i. ANGELIA ANN[8] LIGHTSEY was born on 12 Nov 1973 in Appling County, Georgia. She
    married William Ashley Kearney, son of Bill Kearney and Delynda (unknown) on 20
    Oct 2001 in Appling County, Georgia. He was born on 11 Aug 1976 in Wayne County,
    Georgia.

25. ii. ANNETTE DELAINE LIGHTSEY was born on 24 Apr 1964 in Jacksonville, Florida. She
    married Roy R. Robson on 28 Jun 1985 in Appling County, Georgia. He was born on
    04 Sep 1963 in Selma, Alabama.

19. **KENNETH LEE[7] SELLERS** (Pauline[6] Turner, Albert Oliver[5] Turner, William Franklin[4] Turner, James
Jarrett[3] Turner, Jarrett[2] Turner, Micajah[1] Turner) was born on 10 Apr 1958 in Appling County,
Georgia. He died on 18 Jul 2004 in Savannah, Georgia. He married **KAREN KESSEL**. She was
born on 15 Aug 1961.

Kenneth Lee Sellers and Karen Kessel had the following children:

  i. BREANNA[8] SELLERS.

  ii. HEATHER SELLERS.

20. **DONNA PATRICIA[7] SELLERS** (Pauline[6] Turner, Albert Oliver[5] Turner, William Franklin[4] Turner,
James Jarrett[3] Turner, Jarrett[2] Turner, Micajah[1] Turner) was born on 05 Mar 1965. She married
JOHN HODGES. He was born on 07 Aug 1961.

John Hodges and Donna Patricia Sellers had the following child:

  i. ALANA PATRICIA[8] HODGES was born on 02 Aug 1993.

Generation 8

21. **MARK Edward[8] SIMMONS** (Edward Wilton[7], Monteen[6] Turner, Albert Oliver[5] Turner, William
Franklin[4] Turner, James Jarrett[3] Turner, Jarrett[2] Turner, Micajah[1] Turner) was born on 29 Oct
1967. He married (1) **DIANA GAIL EDWARDS** on 23 Dec 1988 in Plant City, Florida. She was born
on 28 Mar 1969 in Plant City, Florida. He married **SHERRI (UNKNOWN)**. He married **NANCY SANTIAGO**

CLARIDY.

Mark Edward Simmons and Diana Gail Edwards had the following children:

    i. MARK GREGORY[9] EDWARDS was born on 20 Jun 1988 in Plant City, Florida. He married Julie Ann Mercer on 17 Feb 2007 in Wellston, Ohio. She was born on 28 May 1988.

    ii. DAVIAN GAIL SIMMONS was born on 12 Feb 1991 in Monroe, North Carolina. She married Jerrod Elden Rogers, son of James J. Rogers and Betty Lou Eberts on 24 Mar 2012 in Berlin Crossroads, Jackson County, Ohio. He was born on 17 Mar 1987 in Ohio.

Mark Edward Simmons and Sherri (unknown) had the following child:

    iii. MARISSA DAWN (UNKNOWN) was born on 11 Aug 1987. She married JARED REEVES. He was born on 28 Feb 1988.

Mark Edward Simmons and Nancy Santiago Claridy had the following child:

    iv. ASHLEY NICOLE SIMMONS was born on 21 Oct 1985. She married JUSTIN HELMS. He was born on 26 Jan 1986.

22. MICHELLE[8] TURNER (Billy[7], Talmadge[6], Albert Oliver[5], William Franklin[4], James Jarrett[3], Jarrett[2], Micajah[1]) was born on 18 Jul 1965 in Appling County, Georgia. She married JOHN DARREN HENDERSON. He was born on 18 Nov 1965.

John Darren Henderson and Michelle Turner had the following child:

    i. JENNIFER MICHELLE[9] HENDERSON was born on 19 Apr 1986.

23. KENDRA LENEA[8] EASON (Elaine[7] Carter, Irene[6] Turner, Albert Oliver[5] Turner, William Franklin[4] Turner, James Jarrett[3] Turner, Jarrett[2] Turner, Micajah[1] Turner) was born on 20 Dec 1966 in Bacon County, Georgia. She died on 29 Dec 1989 in Appling County, Georgia. She married Jeffery Johnson on 21 Sep 1986 in Appling County, Georgia. He was born in Appling County, Georgia.

More About Kendra LeNea Eason:

Burial: Appling County, Georgia

Jeffery Johnson and Kendra LeNea Eason had the following child:

    i. TREVOR LEE[9] JOHNSON was born on 16 Sep 1987 in Appling County, Georgia.

24. ANGELIA ANN[8] LIGHTSEY (Eileen[7] Carter, Irene[6] Turner, Albert Oliver[5] Turner, William Franklin[4] Turner, James Jarrett[3] Turner, Jarrett[2] Turner, Micajah[1] Turner) was born on 12 Nov 1973 in Appling County, Georgia. She married William Ashley Kearney, son of Bill Kearney and Delynda (unknown) on 20 Oct 2001 in Appling County, Georgia. He was born on 11 Aug 1976 in Wayne County, Georgia.

William Ashley Kearney and Angelia Ann Lightsey had the following child:

    i. LAUREN[9] KEARNEY.

25. ANNETTE DELAINE[8] LIGHTSEY (Eileen[7] Carter, Irene[6] Turner, Albert Oliver[5] Turner, William Franklin[4] Turner, James Jarrett[3] Turner, Jarrett[2] Turner, Micajah[1] Turner) was born on 24 Apr 1964 in Jacksonville, Florida. She married Roy R. Robson on 28 Jun 1985 in Appling County, Georgia. He was born on 04 Sep 1963 in Selma, Alabama.

Roy R. Robson and Annette Delaine Lightsey had the following children:

    i. BROOKE LENEA[9] ROBSON was born on 25 Mar 1984 in Wayne County, Georgia.

More About Brooke LeNea Robson:
Military Service: 21 Sep 2004; U. S. Army

ii.   JAMES ROY ROBSON was born on 01 Sep 1986 in Wayne County, Georgia.

Descendants of Jacob Canup

Generation 1

1. JACOB[1] CANUP was born about 1815 in North Carolina. He died in 1896. He married MARY ANN CROW. She was born about 1820 in Georgia. She died in 1911.

More About Jacob Canup:
Living In: 1850 District 4, Habersham County, Georgia
Living In: 1860 Habersham County, Georgia
Living In: 1870 Mud Creek District, Habersham County, Georgia
Living In: 1880 Narramore District, Hall County, Georgia
Occupation: 1850 - Millwright
Occupation: 1860 - Millwright and Farmer
Occupation: 1880 - Farmer
Occupation: 1870 – Farmer

Jacob Canup and Mary Ann Crow had the following children:

 i. JOHN MONROE[2] CANUP was born on 10 Jun 1841 in Habersham County, Georgia. He died on 17 Mar 1911 in Georgia. He married Mary Miranda Ferguson, daughter of Andrew Jackson Ferguson and Jane Higgins on 17 Jul 1866 in Habersham County, Georgia. She was born on 17 Mar 1846 in Georgia. She died on 17 Apr 1931 in Habersham County, Georgia.

 ii. F. M. CANUP was born about 1842 in Habersham County, Georgia.

 iii. MARGARET CAROLINE CANUP was born about 1845 in Habersham County, Georgia. She died on 03 Jan 1914. She married WILLIAM JACKSON FERGUSON. He was born on 17 Mar 1841 in Georgia. He died on 20 May 1924 in Towns County, Georgia.

 iv. SARAH JANE CANUP was born about 1847 in Habersham County, Georgia.

3. v. WILLIAM W. CANUP was born in May 1848 in Habersham County, Georgia. He married MARY D. (UNKNOWN). She was born in Aug 1863 in Georgia.

 vi. MILES D. CANUP was born about 1851 in Habersham County, Georgia.

 vii. JACOB C. CANUP was born about 1854 in Habersham County, Georgia.

 viii. AMANDA M. CANUP was born about 1857 in Habersham County, Georgia.

 ix. MATTHEW H. CANUP was born about 1858 in Habersham County, Georgia.

 x. CICERO CANUP was born about 1860 in Habersham County, Georgia.

iii. xi. NEWTON JAMES CANUP was born on 03 Jun 1864 in Habersham County, Georgia. He died on 31 Aug 1936 in Appling County, Georgia. He married Nancy Amanda Jenkins, daughter of John Jenkins and Elizabeth (unknown) on 11 Mar 1889 in Hall County, Georgia. She was born in May 1875 in Hall County, Georgia. She died in Appling County, Georgia.

Generation 2

2 WILLIAM W.[2] CANUP (Jacob[1]) was born in May 1848 in Habersham County, Georgia. He married MARY D. (UNKNOWN). She was born in Aug 1863 in Georgia.

William W. Canup and Mary D. (unknown) had the following child:

PINCNEY L.[3] CANUP was born in Jun 1899 in Georgia.

3. **NEWTON JAMES**[2] **CANUP** (Jacob[1]) was born on 03 Jun 1864 in Habersham County, Georgia. He died on 31 Aug 1936 in Appling County, Georgia. He married Nancy Amanda Jenkins, daughter of John Jenkins and Elizabeth (unknown) on 11 Mar 1889 in Hall County, Georgia. She was born in May 1875 in Hall County, Georgia. She died in Appling County, Georgia.

More About Newton James Canup:
Living In: 1900   Narramore District, Hall County, Georgia
Living In: 1920   Nanramore District, Hall County, Georgia
Living In: 1930   Appling County, Georgia
Occupation: Farmer

Newton James Canup and Nancy Amanda Jenkins had the following children:

4.   i. CORA LEE[3] CANUP was born on 24 Dec 1890 in Hall County, Georgia. She died on 22 Aug 1980 in Baxley, Georgia. She married WILLIAM FRANKLIN TURNER. He was born on 03 Jul 1861 in Union County, Georgia. He died on 20 Aug 1919 in Banks County, Georgia. She married DAVID CHAPMAN CARTER. He was born on 10 Aug 1890. He died on 30 Dec 1966 in Jeff Davis County, Georgia.

         ii. NORA CANUP was born on 26 Dec 1894 in Georgia. She died on 27 Mar 1962 in Wayne County, Georgia. She married JOHN HENRY JENKINS. He was born on 15 Jul 1874 in Hall County, Georgia. He died on 02 Jun 1959 in Appling County, Georgia.

         iii.

         More About Nora Canup:
         Burial: Pleasant Grove Cemetery, Appling County,
         Georgia
         Living In: 1962 in Appling County, Georgia

5.   iii. LOUSIANA CANUP was born on 19 Aug 1896 in Hall County, Georgia. She died on 25 Apr 1965 in Baxley, Georgia. She married Albert Oliver Turner, son of William Franklin Turner and Vada Payne in Hall County, Georgia. He was born on 03 Feb 1897 in Hall County, Georgia. He died on 29 Sep 1976 in Chatham County, Georgia.

Generation 3

4. **CORA LEE**[3] **CANUP** (Newton James[2], Jacob[1]) was born on 24 Dec 1890 in Hall County, Georgia. She died on 22 Aug 1980 in Baxley, Georgia. She married **WILLIAM FRANKLIN TURNER**. He was born on 03 Jul 1861 in Union County, Georgia. He died on 20 Aug 1919 in Banks County, Georgia. She married **DAVID CHAPMAN CARTER**. He was born on 10 Aug 1890. He died on 30 Dec 1966 in Jeff Davis County, Georgia.

More About Cora Lee Canup:
Burial: 24 Aug 1980 in Ten Mile Creek Baptist Church Cemetery, Baxley, Appling County, Georgia
Living In: 1920 Cora and her children are living with her parents in Narramore District, Hall County, Georgia

More About William Franklin Turner:
Living In: 1900 Polksville District, Hall County, Georgia

Occupation: ; Farmer

William Franklin Turner and Cora Lee Canup had the following children:

  i. ROBERT NEWTON[4] TURNER was born on 21 Apr 1909 in Hall County, Georgia. He died on 27 Mar 1980 in Baxley, Georgia. He married Maybell C. Carter, daughter of Chatman Carter and Lula Sapp on 29 Oct 1929. She was born on 28 May 1911. She died on 26 Jan 1996 in Appling County, Georgia.

  ii. MAMIE L. TURNER was born on 17 Nov 1910 in Banks County, Georgia. She died on 6 Jan 1998 in Baxley, Georgia. She married LLOYD G. STEEDLEY. He was born on 27 Jul 1898 in Appling County, Georgia. He died on 22 Dec 1956 in Appling County, Georgia.

  More About Mamie L. Turner:
  Burial: Appling County, Georgia

MAGGIE BEATRICE TURNER was born on 26 Nov 1912 in Banks County, Georgia. She died on 10 Mar 1983 in Glynn County, Georgia. She married CLARENCE EARVIN CHASTEEN. He was born in Appling County, Georgia. He died on 16 Dec 1965 in Glynn County, Georgia.

  More About Maggie Beatrice Turner:
  Burial: Appling County, Georgia

ELDORA TURNER was born about 1914 in Banks County, Georgia. She died about 1926 in Hall County, Georgia.

 6. v. MOENA LEVADA TURNER was born on 27 Apr 1917 in Banks County, Georgia. She married HERMAN JAMES COBIA. He was born on 11 Feb 1919 in Eastman, Georgia. He died on 05 May 1970 in Gulfport, Mississippi.

  vi. JOHN HENRY TURNER was born on 01 Feb 1920 in Hall County, Georgia. He died on 12 Oct 2002 in Appling County, Georgia. He married BEATRICE WEAVER. He married VERDIE MAE HUGHES. She was born in 1938 in Georgia. She died in 1955 in Appling County, Georgia.

  More About John Henry Turner:
  Burial: Old Pleasant Grove Cemetery, Baxley, Georgia

More About David Chapman Carter:
Burial: Ten Mile Creek Baptist Church Cemetery, Baxley, Appling County, Georgia
Living In: 1966 Appling County, Georgia

5. LOUSIANA[3] CANUP (Newton James[2], Jacob[1]) was born on 19 Aug 1896 in Hall County, Georgia. She died on 25 Apr 1965 in Baxley, Georgia. She married Albert Oliver Turner, son of William Franklin Turner and Vada Payne in Hall County, Georgia. He was born on 03 Feb 1897 in Hall County, Georgia. He died on 29 Sep 1976 in Chatham County, Georgia.

More About Lousiana Canup:
Burial: 27 Apr 1965 in Old Pleasant Grove Cemetery, Appling County, Georgia
Occupation: 1920; Works on horse farm

Notes for Lousiana Canup:
Used Lucy instead of Lousiana for given name.
Family members remember her maiden name as Canup. Funeral home records show her parents as Amanda Jenkins and Tom Bryant.

More About Albert Oliver Turner:
Burial: Old Pleasant Grove Cemetery, Appling County, Georgia
Living In: 1900 Polksville District, Hall County, Georgia
Living In: 1920 Narramore District, Hall County, Georgia
Living In: 1930 Appling County, Georgia
Living In: 1976 Baxley, Georgia
Occupation: Farmer

Notes for Albert Oliver Turner:
World War One draft registration gives birth date as February 3, 1897. Headstone gives birth date as January 3, 1899. Birth date in 1900 Federal census is January 1897. Social security death index gives birthdate as January 3, 1899.

Albert Oliver Turner and Lousiana Canup had the following children:

7.   i.   MONTEEN[4] TURNER was born on 28 Feb 1916 in Hall County, Georgia. She died on 16 Jun 1984 in Brunswick, Georgia. She married EDWARD SIMMONS. He was born about 1912 in Georgia.

8.   ii.   TALMADGE TURNER was born on 27 Sep 1917 in Hall County, Georgia. He died on 16 Aug 1983 in Baxley, Georgia. He married Inez Altman on 08 Jan 1945 in Appling County, Georgia. She was born on 02 Oct 1928 in Georgia. She died on 01 Jul 2007 in Baxley, Georgia.

9.   iii. IRENE TURNER was born on 30 Jun 1922 in Hall County, Georgia. She died on 07 Aug 1988 in Appling County, Georgia. She married James B. Carter, son of James Carter and Allie Sapp on 06 Jun 1942 in Appling County, Georgia. He was born on 29 Mar 1924 in Appling County, Georgia. He died on 29 Jul 2003 in Appling County, Georgia.

10   iv. WILLIAM THOMAS TURNER was born on 10 Nov 1925 in Hall County, Georgia. He died on 05 Aug 2004 in Appling County, Georgia. He married Eleanor Lightsey, daughter of Kenneth Lightsey and Myrtle Tyre in Appling County, Georgia. She was born on 06 Jul 1931 in Appling County, Georgia. She died on 18 Feb 1994 in Appling County, Georgia.

11   v.   PAULINE TURNER was born on 10 Nov 1928 in Appling County, Georgia. She died on Oct 2002 in Appling County, Georgia. She married DWIGHT SELLERS. He was born in Appling County, Georgia.

        vii. INFANT DAUGHTER TURNER.

Generation 4

6.   MOENA LEVADA[4] TURNER (Cora Lee[3] Canup, Newton James[2] Canup, Jacob[1] Canup) was born on 27 Apr 1917 in Banks County, Georgia. She married HERMAN JAMES COBIA. He was born on 11 Feb 1919 in Eastman, Georgia. He died on 05 May 1970 in Gulfport, Mississippi.

More About Herman James Cobia:

Burial: Harrison County, Mississippi

Herman James Cobia and Moena Levada Turner had the following child:

    1.   ELLA MYRTICE[5] COBIA was born on 12 Nov 1940 in Baxley, Georgia.

7.   **MONTEEN[4] TURNER** (Lousiana[3] Canup, Newton James[2] Canup, Jacob[1] Canup) was born on 28 Feb 1916 in Hall County, Georgia. She died on 16 Jun 1984 in Brunswick, Georgia. She married **EDWARD SIMMONS**. He was born about 1912 in Georgia.

More About Monteen Turner:
Burial: 19 Jun 1984 in Pleasant Grove Cemetery, Baxley, Georgia
Living In: 1984 Sterling Community, Glynn County, Georgia
Occupation: Worked thirty years for SeaPak Shrimp Company on St. Simons Island, Glynn County, Georgia

Notes for Monteen Turner:
SIMMONS, Monteen (Turner)
The Brunswick News; Monday 18 June 1984; pg. 3A col. 5

SIMMONS FUNERAL BEING HELD TODAY
Services for Monteen Turner Simmons, 68, a resident of Sterling who died early Saturday at the Glynn-Brunswick Memorial Hospital after a short illness will be held Tuesday.
She was a native of Appling County and had been a resident of Glynn County for the past 35 years. She had been employed by Sea-Pak for the past 30 years. She was a member of the Holiness Church in Baxley.
She is survived by two daughters, Willene Lott of St. Simons and Lulene Tison of Sterling. Two sons, Edward W. Simmons of Plant City, Fla. and Gary Simmons of Sterling; two sisters, Irene Carter of Baxley and Pauline Sellers of Savannah; a brother Bill Turner of Baxley; seven grandchildren; two great-grandchildren; several nieces and nephews.
Services will be held Tuesday at 1 p.m. in the chapel of Edo Miller & Sons Funeral with the Rev. Dorris Black officiating. Entombment services will be held at 3:30 p.m. in Pleasant Grove Cemetery near Baxley.
The family will receive friends at the funeral home tonight from 6 until 9 o'clock. Edo Miller & Sons Funeral Home is in charge of arrangements.

More About Edward Simmons:
Living In: 1920 Surrency, Georgia
Living In: 1930 Deems, Georgia

Edward Simmons and Monteen Turner had the following children:

    i.   EDWARD WILTON[5] SIMMONS was born on 29 Aug 1935 in Georgia. He died on 23 Apr 1997 in Hillsborough County, Florida. He married LEONA RYALS. She was born on 14 Aug 1939 in Georgia.

        More About Edward Wilton Simmons:
        Burial: Hopewell Memorial Gardens, Plant City, Florida

    ii.   WILLEEN SIMMONS. She married ARCHIE LOTT.

    iii.   LULLEEN SIMMONS. She married BUTCH TISON.

4   GARY SIMMONS was born in Glynn County, Georgia.

5   INFANT DAUGHTER SIMMONS was born on 14 Jul 1956 in Glynn County, Georgia. She died on 14 Jul 1956.

6

Notes   for   Infant   Daughter
Simmons: Lived for ten minutes.

8.   **TALMADGE**[4] **TURNER** (Lousiana[3] Canup, Newton James[2] Canup, Jacob[1] Canup) was born on 27 Sep 1917 in Hall County, Georgia. He died on 16 Aug 1983 in Baxley, Georgia. He married Inez Altman on 08 Jan 1945 in Appling County, Georgia. She was born on 02 Oct 1928 in Georgia. She died on 01 Jul 2007 in Baxley, Georgia.

More About Talmadge Turner:
Burial: Old Pleasant Grove Cemetery, Appling County, Georgia

More About Inez Altman:
Burial: Old Pleasant Grove Cemetery, Appling County, Georgia

Talmadge Turner and Inez Altman had the following child:

    i.   BILLY[5] TURNER was born on 28 Mar 1946 in Appling County, Georgia. He married Virginia (unknown) in Appling County, Georgia.

9.   **IRENE**[4] **TURNER** (Lousiana[3] Canup, Newton James[2] Canup, Jacob[1] Canup) was born on 30 Jun 1922 in Hall County, Georgia. She died on 07 Aug 1988 in Appling County, Georgia. She married James B. Carter, son of James Carter and Allie Sapp on 06 Jun 1942 in Appling County, Georgia. He was born on 29 Mar 1924 in Appling County, Georgia. He died on 29 Jul 2003 in Appling County, Georgia.

More About Irene Turner: Burial:
Appling County, Georgia

More About James B. Carter:
Burial: 31 Jul 2003 in Appling County, Georgia
Occupation: Sheriff of Appling County, Georgia August 1960-1976
Occupation: Chief of Police, Baxley, Georgia, 1976-1979
Military Service: U.S. Army, World War Two

James B. Carter and Irene Turner had the following children:

    i.   ELAINE[5] CARTER was born on 17 Nov 1943. She married (1) RICHARD EASON in Appling County, Georgia. He was born in Appling County, Georgia. She married RONNIE DOWDNEY. He was born on 22 Nov 1946.

    ii.   EILEEN CARTER was born on 21 Sep 1946 in Appling County, Georgia. She died on 15 Sep 2010 in Appling County, Georgia. She married (1) JOE VESTON LIGHTSEY, son of George Lightsey and Senia Pearce in Nov 1963. He was born on 05 Mar 1944 in Appling County, Georgia. She married WAYNE HARRIS.

        More About Eileen Carter:
        Burial: 18 Sep 2010 in Milliken cemetery, Appling County, Georgia
        Occupation: Shipping Supervisor

10.   **WILLIAM THOMAS[4] TURNER** (Lousiana[3] Canup, Newton James[2] Canup, Jacob[1] Canup) was born on 10 Nov 1925 in Hall County, Georgia. He died on 05 Aug 2004 in Appling County, Georgia. He married Eleanor Lightsey, daughter of Kenneth Lightsey and Myrtle Tyre in Appling County, Georgia. She was born on 06 Jul 1931 in Appling County, Georgia. She died on 18 Feb 1994 in Appling County, Georgia.

More About William Thomas Turner:
Burial: 06 Aug 2004 in Pine Grove Freewill Baptist Church, Appling County, Georgia

More About Eleanor Lightsey:
Burial: Pine Grove Freewill Baptist Church, Appling County, Georgia

William Thomas Turner and Eleanor Lightsey had the following children:

    i.   JOAN[5] TURNER was born on 06 Aug 1949 in Appling County, Georgia. She died on 18 Feb 1951 in Appling County, Georgia.

       More About Joan Turner:
       Burial: Pine Grove Freewill Baptist Church, Appling County, Georgia

    2.   WILLIAM TERRY TURNER was born on 19 Mar 1956.

    3.   SANDY TURNER was born on 23 Jun 1974.

11.   **PAULINE[4] TURNER** (Lousiana[3] Canup, Newton James[2] Canup, Jacob[1] Canup) was born on 10 Nov 1928 in Appling County, Georgia. She died on 29 Oct 2002 in Appling County, Georgia. She married **DWIGHT SELLERS**. He was born in Appling County, Georgia.

More About Pauline Turner:
Burial: 01 Nov 2002 in Zion Baptist Church Cemetery, Appling County, Georgia

Dwight Sellers and Pauline Turner had the following children:

    i.   JUNE[5] SELLERS was born in 1955 in Appling County, Georgia.

    ii.   KENNETH LEE SELLERS was born on 10 Apr 1958 in Appling County, Georgia. He died on 18 Jul 2004 in Savannah, Georgia. He married KAREN KESSEL. She was born on 15 Aug 1961.

    iii.   DONNA PATRICIA SELLERS was born on 05 Mar 1965. She married JOHN HODGES. He was born on 07 Aug 1961.

Notes:

Descendants of Thomas H. Johnson

Generation 1

1. **THOMAS H.**[1] **JOHNSON** was born about 1834 in North Carolina. He died about 1879 in Appling County, Georgia. He married Courtney Jones, daughter of Theophilus Jones and Zylphia Hutto on 29 Mar 1866 in Dooly County, Georgia. She was born on 22 Apr 1839 in Dooley County, Georgia. She died on 08 Feb 1932 in Appling County, Georgia.

More About Thomas H. Johnson:
Living In: 1870 Mitchell County, Georgia
Occupation: 1870 - Farm Labor

Notes for Thomas H. Johnson:
Birth year is from 1870 U.S. census.

More About Courtney Jones:
Burial: Bethel Free Will Baptist Church Cemetery, Appling County, Georgia
Living In: 1860 With her parents in Dooly County, Georgia
Living In: 1880 Widow in Dooly County, Georgia

Notes for Courtney Jones:
1860 and 1870 U. S. census reports indicate a birth date of about 1847. 1880 U.S. census gives a birth year of 1843.

Thomas H. Johnson and Courtney Jones had the following children:

  i. JAMES HENRY[2] JOHNSON was born on 08 Nov 1867 in Georgia. He died on 20 Aug 1930 in Kirkland, Georgia. He married SARAH E. (UNKNOWN). She was born in 1875. She died in 1955.

  More About James Henry Johnson:
  Burial: 21 Aug 1930 in Antioch Baptist Church Cemetery, Kirkland, Georgia
  Occupation: Farmer

  ii. THOMAS JOHNSON was born about 1872 in Georgia.

2. iii. NANCY ANN JOHNSON was born on 11 Feb 1873 in Dooley County, Georgia. She died on 13 Feb 1966 in Appling County, Georgia. She married Benjamin Franklin Simmons about 1897. He was born in Jan 1872 in Georgia. He died between 08 Jan 1920-14 Apr 1930.

3. iv. ZYLPHIA HENRIETTA JOHNSON was born on 01 Jan 1874 in Georgia. She died on 30 Nov 1941 in Ware County, Georgia. She married JAMES ELIZAH JONES. He was born on 21 Jan 1874 in Appling County, Georgia. He died on 12 Jul 1937 in Ware County, Georgia.

  v. LEOLA JOHNSON was born on 22 Apr 1878 in Georgia. She died on 15 Sep 1970 in Brunswick. Georgia.

4. vi. JOSEPH JOHNSON was born on 25 Jun 1879 in Georgia. He died on 11 Sep 1952 in Georgia. He married RUTH ELIZABETH HARDEN. She was born on 09 Feb 1888 in Georgia. She died on 06 Mar 1926 in Appling County, Georgia.

Generation 2

2. **NANCY ANN**[2] **JOHNSON** (Thomas H.[1]) was born on 11 Feb 1873 in Dooley County, Georgia. She died on 13 Feb 1966 in Appling County, Georgia. She married Benjamin Franklin Simmons about 1897. He was born in Jan 1872 in Georgia. He died between 08 Jan 1920-14 Apr 1930.

More About Nancy Ann Johnson:
Burial: Ten Mile Creek Baptist Church Cemetery, Appling County, Georgia
Living In: 1930 As a widow in Deems, Appling County, Georgia

Notes for Nancy Ann Johnson:
Birth and death dates are from Ten Mile Creek Baptist Church Cemetery. Georgia death index gives birth year as 1873 and date of death as February 13, 1966.

More About Benjamin Franklin Simmons:
Living In: 1900   Rabbitville, Clinch County, Georgia
Living In: 1910 Graham, Appling County, Georgia
Living In: 1920   Surrency, Appling County, Georgia
Occupation: Farmer

Benjamin Franklin Simmons and Nancy Ann Johnson had the following children:

i.   MAUDE BETHEL[3] SIMMONS was born on 22 Feb 1899 in Georgia. She married Forest S. Sapp on 30 May 1929 in Appling County, Georgia. He was born about 1909 in Georgia.

ii.   HARVEY WESLEY SIMMONS was born on 22 Sep 1902 in Georgia.

iii.   BERTIE EVELYN SIMMONS was born on 27 Sep 1904 in Appling County, Georgia. She died on 20 Nov 1934 in Deens, Appling County, Georgia. She married John James Crews on 22 Mar 1926 in Appling County, Georgia. He was born on 26 Sep 1906 in Baker County, Florida. He died on 14 Dec 1963 in Charlton County, Georgia.

iv.   BEULAH VICTORIA SIMMONS was born on 15 Jan 1906 in Georgia. She died on 26 Nov 1973 in Georgia. She married C. M. Turner on 19 Aug 1933 in Appling County, Georgia.

More About Beulah Victoria Simmons:
Burial: Ten Mile Creek Baptist Church Cemetery, Appling County, Georgia

v.   JESSIE GERTRUDE SIMMONS was born on 27 Jan 1907 in Baxley, Appling County, Georgia. She died on 20 Oct 1970 in Brunswick, Georgia. She married ROBERT TURNER.

vi.   RILLA ROSSETER SIMMONS was born on 12 Sep 1909 in Appling County, Georgia. She died on 13 Jan 1988 in Brunswick, Georgia. She married John Lewis Godley on 03 Jul 1938 in Camden, Georgia. He was born on 05 Dec 1907 in Camden, Georgia. He died on 17 May 2003 in Brunswick, Georgia.

More About Rilla Rosseter Simmons:
Burial: Palmetto Cemetery, Brunswick, Georgia

vii.   FRANCES MAE SIMMONS was born about 1911 in Georgia.

8   EDWARD SIMMONS was born about 1912 in Georgia. He married MONTEEN TURNER. She was born on 28 Feb 1916 in Hall County, Georgia. She died on 16 Jun 1984 in Brunswick, Georgia.

   More About Edward Simmons:
   Living In: 1920 Surrency, Georgia
   Living In: 1930 Deems, Georgia

9   WILLIS C. SIMMONS was born about 1915 in Georgia.

10   BENJAMIN F. SIMMONS was born about Jun 1916 in Georgia. He died in 1934.

11   ELIZABETH V. SIMMONS was born about Apr 1919 in Georgia.

3.   ZYLPHIA HENRIETTA[2] JOHNSON (Thomas H.[1]) was born on 01 Jan 1874 in Georgia. She died on 30 Nov 1941 in Ware County, Georgia. She married JAMES ELIZAH JONES. He was born on 21 Jan 1874 in Appling County, Georgia. He died on 12 Jul 1937 in Ware County, Georgia.

More About Zylphia Henrietta Johnson:
Burial: Friendship Freewill Baptist Church Cemetery, Millwood, Ware County, Georgia

More About James Elizah Jones:
Burial: Friendship Freewill Baptist Church Cemetery, Millwood, Ware County, Georgia
Military Service: Company L, 3rd U.S. Volunteer Infantry, Spanish American War

James Elizah Jones and Zylphia Henrietta Johnson had the following children:

   i.   THOMAS E.[3] JONES was born in 1897. He died in 1959.

   ii.   MARVIN K. JONES was born in 1911. He died in 1972.

4.   JOSEPH[2] JOHNSON (Thomas H.[1]) was born on 25 Jun 1879 in Georgia. He died on 11 Sep 1952 in Georgia. He married RUTH ELIZABETH HARDEN. She was born on 09 Feb 1888 in Georgia. She died on 06 Mar 1926 in Appling County, Georgia.

More About Joseph Johnson:
Burial: Bethel Freewill Baptist Church Cemetery, Appling County, Georgia
Living In: 1910 Graham, Appling County, Georgia
Living In: 1920 Graham, Appling County, Georgia
Occupation: Farmer

Notes for Joseph Johnson:
Joseph is not with his mother, Courtney, on the 1880 U.S. census. A number of his relatives believe he is a son of Thomas H. Johnson and Courtney Jones. 1910 U.S. census gives a birth year of Abt.1882. 1920 U.S. census gives a birth year of Abt. 1881. Having a daughter named Zylphia could indicate a connection with Courtney Jones, who had a daughter named Zylphia and Courtney's mother, who was named Zylphia.

More About Ruth Elizabeth Harden:
Burial: Bethel Freewill Baptist Church Cemetery, Appling County, Georgia

Notes for Ruth Elizabeth Harden:
Death certificate has February 9, 1888 as date of birth. Cemetery has February 15, 1888 as date of birth.

Joseph Johnson and Ruth Elizabeth Harden had the following children:

1.   FRANCIS[3] JOHNSON was born about 1904 in Georgia.

2.   WALTER JOHNSON was born about 1905 in Georgia.

3.   ALLEN JOHNSON was born about Dec 1908 in Georgia.

4.   JOSEPHINE JOHNSON was born about Mar 1910 in Georgia.

5.   ZYLPHIA JOHNSON was born about 1911 in Georgia.

6.   BETTIE JOHNSON was born about 1913 in Georgia.

7.   LILA JOHNSON was born about 1915 in Georgia.

8.   J. C. JOHNSON was born about 1917 in Georgia.

Descendants of Jabez D. Ryals

Generation 1

2. **JABEZ D.**[1] **RYALS** was born about 1826 in Georgia. He died on 01 Aug 1904 in Georgia. He married **SARAH AMOS**. She was born about 1835 in Georgia. She died on 16 May 1906 in Georgia.

More About Jabez D. Ryals:
Burial: Plum Orchard Cemetery, Cox, McIntosh County, Georgia
Living In: 1850 McIntosh County, Georgia
Living In: 1860 McIntosh County, Georgia
Living In: 1870 McIntosh County, Georgia
Living In: 1880 Darien, McIntosh County, Georgia
Living In: 1900 Barrington, McIntosh County, Georgia
Military Service: May 21, 1862 - May 17, 1864, Company K, 5th Georgia Cavalry, C.S.A.

Notes for Jabez D. Ryals:
Jabez was 36 years old on May 21, 1862 when he was mustered in with the First Battalion of Georgia Cavalry which was later part of the 5th Regiment of Georgia Cavalry.

More About Sarah Amos:
Burial: Plum Orchard Cemetery, Cox, McIntosh County, Georgia

Jabez D. Ryals and Sarah Amos had the following children:

    i.   RUTH[2] RYALS was born about 1849 in Georgia.

    ii.   CATHERINE RYALS was born about 1852 in Georgia.

    iii.   MADISON RYALS was born about 1855 in Georgia.

    iv.   LAVINIA RYALS was born about 1857 in Georgia.

3.   v. BEAUREGARD RYALS was born in 1861 in Georgia. He died in 1934 in Georgia. He married NETTIE J. (UNKNOWN). She was born in 1870. She died in 1935.

    xi.   MARY RYALS was born about 1862 in Georgia.

iii.   vii. ISRAEL RYALS was born on 08 Mar 1866 in Georgia. He died on 03 Nov 1949 in Georgia. He married MINNIE (UNKNOWN). She was born on 15 Oct 1872 in Georgia. She died on 16 Apr 1943 in Georgia.

    SERAPHA RYALS was born about 1870 in Georgia.

iv.   ix. SMITH RYALS was born on 23 Dec 1871 in Georgia. He died on 15 Apr 1946 in McIntosh County, Georgia. He married Annie Laura Howard, daughter of (unknown) Howard and (unknown) in 1894. She was born on 23 Dec 1874 in Georgia. She died on 05 Jan 1942 in Georgia.

Generation 2

3 **BEAUREGARD**[2] **RYALS** (Jabez D.[1]) was born in 1861 in Georgia. He died in 1934 in Georgia. He married **NETTIE J. (UNKNOWN)**. She was born in 1870. She died in 1935.

More About Beauregard Ryals:
Burial: Hardshell Baptist Church Cemetery, Darien, McIntosh County, Georgia

Living In: 1900 Barrington, McIntosh County, Georgia

More About Nettie J. (unknown):
Burial: Hardshell Baptist Church Cemetery, Darien, McIntosh County, Georgia

Beauregard Ryals and Nettie J. (unknown) had the following children:

      i. RUCIAN DETROIT[3] RYALS was born on 13 Nov 1893. He died on 08 Jan 1932. He married MARGARET B ROWARD HURLBERT. She was born on 19 Feb 1905 in Duval County, Florida. She died on 05 Jan 1932.

        More About Rucian Detroit Ryals:
        Burial: Evergreen Cemetery, Jacksonville, Florida

      ii. KESLER RYALS was born in Feb 1896 in Georgia.

      iii. MABEL RYALS was born in Mar 1898 in Georgia.

3. ISRAEL[2] RYALS (Jabez D.[1]) was born on 08 Mar 1866 in Georgia. He died on 03 Nov 1949 in Georgia. He married MINNIE (UNKNOWN). She was born on 15 Oct 1872 in Georgia. She died on 16 Apr 1943 in Georgia.

More About Israel Ryals:
Burial: Hardshell Baptist Church Cemetery, Darien, McIntosh County, Georgia
Living In: 1900 Barrington, McIntosh County, Georgia

More About Minnie (unknown):
Burial: Hardshell Baptist Church Cemetery, Darien, McIntosh County, Georgia

Israel Ryals and Minnie (unknown) had the following children:

      i. JABEZ[3] RYALS was born in Feb 1892 in Georgia.

      ii. SARAH RYALS was born in Feb 1894 in Georgia.

      iii. MINNIE RYALS was born in May 1896 in Georgia.

      iv. HANNAH RYALS was born in Jan 1898 in Georgia.

4. SMITH[2] RYALS (Jabez D.[1]) was born on 23 Dec 1871 in Georgia. He died on 15 Apr 1946 in McIntosh County, Georgia. He married Annie Laura Howard, daughter of (unknown) Howard and (unknown) in 1894. She was born on 23 Dec 1874 in Georgia. She died on 05 Jan 1942 in Georgia.

More About Smith Ryals:
Burial: Hardshell Baptist Church Cemetery, Darien, McIntosh County, Georgia
Living In: 1880 Darien, Georgia
Living In: 1900 Barrington, McIntosh County, Georgia
Living In: 1910 McIntosh County, Georgia
Living In: 1920 Barrington, McIntosh County, Georgia
Living In: 1930 Jones, McIntosh County, Georgia
Occupation: 1900;Farmer

More About Annie Laura Howard:

Burial: Hardshell Baptist Church Cemetery, Darien, McIntosh County, Georgia

Smith Ryals and Annie Laura Howard had the following children:

i. REUBEN L.[3] RYALS was born on 10 Oct 1895 in Georgia. He died on 04 Nov 1967 in Georgia.

More About Reuben L. Ryals:
Burial: Hardshell Baptist Church Cemetery, Darien, McIntosh County, Georgia

2. EPHRAIM RYALS was born on 30 Jan 1896 in Georgia. He died on 31 Jan 1966 in Georgia.

More About Ephraim Ryals:
Burial: Hardshell Baptist Church Cemetery, Darien, McIntosh County, Georgia Military Service: Quartermaster Corps, World War One

3. BETTY RYALS was born in Feb 1899 in Georgia.

4. LUTHER RYALS was born about 1901 in Georgia.

5. JESLO RYALS was born on 11 Feb 1905 in Georgia. He died in May 1960 in Georgia.

More About Jeslo Ryals:
Burial: Hardshell Baptist Church Cemetery, Darien, McIntosh County, Georgia

6. FREDDY RYALS was born about 1907 in Georgia.

7. BERTHA RYALS was born about Dec 1909 in Georgia.

5. viii. GRIMSHAW RYALS was born on 25 May 1913 in Liberty County, Georgia. He died on 13 Aug 1990 in Richmond County, Georgia. He married TULLUE DEAL. She was born on 15 Aug 1912 in Georgia. She died on 02 Mar 2006 in Florida.

ix. MORRIS RYALS was born about 1914 in Georgia.

Generation 3

5. GRIMSHAW[3] RYALS (Smith[2], Jabez D.[1]) was born on 25 May 1913 in Liberty County, Georgia. He died on 13 Aug 1990 in Richmond County, Georgia. He married TULLUE DEAL. She was born on 15 Aug 1912 in Georgia. She died on 02 Mar 2006 in Florida.

More About Grimshaw Ryals:
Burial: Hardshell Baptist Church Cemetery, Darien, McIntosh County, Georgia
Living In: 1920   Barrington, Georgia
Living In: 1990 Blythe, Georgia
Occupation: 1913; Truck Driver
Military Service: 14 Dec 1944; Enlisted in U.S. Army at Fort McPherson, Georgia.

More About Tullue Deal:
Burial: Hopewell Memorial Gardens, Plant City, Hillsborough County, Florida

Notes for Tullue Deal:
Social Security death index gives a birth date of August 15, 1911.
Buried next to her son, Grimshaw.

Grimshaw Ryals and Tullue Deal had the following children:

6.　　i. KENNETH[4] RYALS was born on 13 Apr 1937 in Savannah. Georgia. He died on 09 Apr 2008 in Brunswick, Georgia. He married BARBARA LUCILLE MUMFORD. She was born on 23 Oct 1942. She died on 01 Oct 1989 in Brunswick, Georgia. He married MARGARET HIGHSMITH.

　　ii GRIMSHAW RYALS was born on 24 Mar 1944 in Savannah, Georgia. He died on 07　Mar 2004 in Plant City, Florida.

　　　More About Grimshaw Ryals:
　　　Burial: 10 Mar 2004 in Hopewell Memorial Gardens, Plant City, Florida

　　　Notes for Grimshaw Ryals:
　　　Buried next to his mother.

7.　　iii. EVA JUANITA RYALS was born on 09 Dec 1948 in Georgia. She died on 26 Jun 2010 in Plant City, Florida. She married John Lloyd Williams about 1978.

　　iv.　HIRAM RYALS.

8.　　v. LEONA RYALS was born on 14 Aug 1939 in Georgia. She married EDWARD WILTON SIMMONS. He was born on 29 Aug 1935 in Georgia. He died on 23 Apr 1997 in Hillsborough County, Florida. She married (2) JAMES WILLIE WELLS on 24 Apr 2011 in Plant City, Florida. He was born on 10 Aug 1936 in South Carolina. She married ALBERT J. DAVIS.

9.　　vi. EUGENE RYALS was born in 1950. He married CAROL HESTER YARBROUGH. She was born in 1952.

Generation 4

6.　**KENNETH[4] RYALS** (Grimshaw[3], Smith[2], Jabez D.[1]) was born on 13 Apr 1937 in Savannah. Georgia. He died on 09 Apr 2008 in Brunswick, Georgia. He married **BARBARA LUCILLE MUMFORD**. She was born on 23 Oct 1942. She died on 01 Oct 1989 in Brunswick, Georgia. He married **MARGARET HIGHSMITH**.

More About Kenneth Ryals:
Burial: Brunswick Memorial Park Cemetery, Brunswick, Glynn County, Georgia
Occupation: Route salesman for Coca-Cola.
Occupation: Owned his own car detailing business

Notes　for　Kenneth
Ryals: Obituary
Kenneth (Kenny) G. Ryals, 70, a resident of Brunswick died Wednesday evening at his residence. Funeral Services will be 10:00 AM Saturday in the chapel of Brunswick Memorial Park Funeral Home with Rev. Wayne Manning officiating. Interment will follow in Brunswick Memorial Park Cemetery. Mr. Ryals was born in Savannah and a resident of Glynn County for 49 years and a prior resident of Cox. He had retired from Coca-Cola where he was a route salesman. He owned

and operated a car detailing business. He was a wonderful husband, father and grand father, and a friend to all. He was an avid Ford owner and was a collector of Ford cars and Coca-Cola memorabilia. He is survived by his wife, Margaret Highsmith Ryals of Brunswick, two daughters, Kimberly (Kim) Waters (Todd) of Brunswick, Shirley Bedford (Mike) of Millington, TN, four step daughters, Vanessa Lee (Harry) of Hoboken, Christine Turner (Bobby) and Lynn Willis (Travis) both of Nahunta, Tina Temples (Terry) of Woodbine, one step son, Max T. Drury (Rachel) of Waverly, two sisters, Leona Simmons and Juanita Williams of Plant City, FL, two brothers, Hiram (Scooter) Ryals (Beverly) of Riverview, FL and Eugene Ryals of Plant City, FL., three grandchildren, thirteen step grandchildren, and four step great grandchildren and several nieces and nephews. He was preceded in death by his first wife, Lucille, his parents, Grimshaw and Tulla Ryals and a brother, Jimmy Ryals. Active pallbearers will be, T. J. Waters, Skippy Howard, Billy Copeland, Steve Pello, Pat Pello, Peter Santiago (Pineapple), Jay Honeycutt and Arthur Sharpe. Honorary pallbearers will be present and former employees of Brunswick Coca-Cola, Staff of third floor St. Vincent Hospital, Dr. Phillip B. Aquila and Staff, Dr. Ossi and First Coast Oncology Staff, Todd Waters, Max Drury, Dr. Robert Thompson and Staff, and Cal Thompson. Family will receive friends from 6:00-8:00 PM Friday, April 11, 2008 at Brunswick Memorial Park Funeral Home. The family request that memorial contributions be made to Hospice of the Golden Isles. Brunswick Memorial Park Funeral Home in charge of arrangements.

More About Barbara Lucille Mumford:
Burial: Brunswick Memorial Park Cemetery, Brunswick, Glynn County, Georgia

Kenneth Ryals and Barbara Lucille Mumford had the following children:

     1   KIMBERLY[5] RYALS.

     2   SHIRLEY RYALS.

7   EVA JUANITA[4] RYALS (Grimshaw[3], Smith[2], Jabez D.[1]) was born on 09 Dec 1948 in Georgia. She died on 26 Jun 2010 in Plant City, Florida. She married John Lloyd Williams about 1978.

More About Eva Juanita Ryals:
Burial: 30 Jun 2010 in Hopewell Memorial Gardens, Plant City, Florida

Notes for Eva Juanita Ryals:
Juanita "Tiny" WILLIAMS
WILLIAMS, Juanita "Tiny," 61, of Plant City, Fla., departed this life June 26, 2010. She was preceded in death by her brothers, Kenneth Ryals and Jimmy Ryals. She is survived by her husband of 32 years, John Lloyd Williams; daughter, Eva Driggs (David); grand-daughter, Amber Owens; siblings, Leona Simmons, Scooter Ryals (Bev), and Eugene Ryals; and many loving family members and friends. A celebration of life will take place at noon Wednesday, June 30, at Hopewell Funeral Home, 6005 State Road 39 S., Plant City, where the family will receive friends at
xi a.m. Interment will follow at Hopewell Memorial Gardens, Plant City. Expressions of condolence may be sent at www.hopewellfuneral.com

John Lloyd Williams and Eva Juanita Ryals had the following child:
     i.   EVA[5] WILLIAMS.

8   LEONA[4] RYALS (Grimshaw[3], Smith[2], Jabez D.[1]) was born on 14 Aug 1939 in Georgia. She married EDWARD WILTON SIMMONS. He was born on 29 Aug 1935 in Georgia. He died on 23 Apr 1997 in Hillsborough County, Florida. She married (2) JAMES WILLIE WELLS on 24 Apr 2011 in Plant City, Florida. He was born on 10 Aug 1936 in South Carolina. She married ALBERT J. DAVIS.

More About Edward Wilton Simmons:
Burial: Hopewell Memorial Gardens, Plant City, Florida

Edward Wilton Simmons and Leona Ryals had the following child:

    i.   MARK EDWARD[5] SIMMONS was born on 29 Oct 1967. He married (1) DIANA GAIL EDWARDS on 23 Dec 1988 in Plant City, Florida. She was born on 28 Mar 1969 in Plant City, Florida. He married SHERRI (UNKNOWN). He married NANCY SANTIAGO CLARIDY.

Albert J. Davis and Leona Ryals had the following child:

    i.   GREG[5] DAVIS.

9.   EUGENE[4] RYALS (Grimshaw[3], Smith[2], Jabez D.[1]) was born in 1950. He married CAROL HESTER YARBROUGH. She was born in 1952.

Eugene Ryals and Carol Hester Yarbrough had the following child:

    1.   SHERRY[5] RYALS.

Descendants of John Deal

1. **JOHN**[1] **DEAL** was born in 1761 in North Carolina. He died in 1818 in Emanuel County, Georgia. He married Mary (unknown) in 1778. She was born in 1754. She died in 1823.

    John Deal and Mary (unknown) had the following child:

    2.   i. SIMON A.[2] DEAL was born in 1779 in North Carolina. He died on 07 Nov 1837 in Emanuel County, Georgia. He married Sintha Williams on 10 Mar 1804 in Bulloch County, Georgia. She was born in 1780 in Bulloch County, Georgia.

Generation 2

2. **SIMON A.**[2] **DEAL** (John[1]) was born in 1779 in North Carolina. He died on 07 Nov 1837 in Emanuel County, Georgia. He married Sintha Williams on 10 Mar 1804 in Bulloch County, Georgia. She was born in 1780 in Bulloch County, Georgia.

    Simon A. Deal and Sintha Williams had the following children:

    SUSAN[3] DEAL was born about 1812.

    JAMES DEAL was born about 1812. He died in 1854.

    iv.   iii. CURTIS DEAL was born about 1814 in North Carolina. He died after 1870 in Georgia. He married Frances Gill on 05 Jul 1835 in Telfair County, Georgia. She was born in 1810 in Tellfair County, Georgia. She died in 1851 in Tellfair County, Georgia.

    iv.   WILLIAM A. DEAL was born about 1816. He died in 1864.

Generation 3

3. **CURTIS**[3] **DEAL** (Simon A.[2], John[1]) was born about 1814 in North Carolina. He died after 1870 in Georgia. He married Frances Gill on 05 Jul 1835 in Telfair County, Georgia. She was born in 1810 in Tellfair County, Georgia. She died in 1851 in Tellfair County, Georgia.

    More About Curtis Deal:
    Burial: Mount Olivet Cemetery, Liberty County, Georgia
    Living In: 1850 Telfair County, Georgia
    Living In: 1860 Liberty County, Georgia
    Living In: 1870 Living with his son John Deal in McIntosh County, Georgia

    Curtis Deal and Frances Gill had the following children:
    SARAH[4] DEAL was born about 1836 in Georgia.

    v.   ii. ZACHARIAH DEAL was born on 24 Feb 1838 in Telfair County, Georgia. He died on 29 Nov 1919 in Liberty County, Georgia. He married Alice Alethea Jackson, daughter of Joseph Jackson and Mary Ann Somersall on 27 Mar 1862. She was born on 27 Oct 1843 in Liberty County, Georgia. She died on 15 Aug 1915 in Darien, McIntosh County, Georgia.

    JACOB J. DEAL was born about 1841 in Georgia.

    CORNELIUS DEAL was born about 1844 in Georgia.

    ELIZA M. DEAL was born about 1845 in Georgia.

    DRUCILLA DEAL was born about 1846 in Georgia. She died in 1900.

5.　　vii. JOHN WASHINGTON DEAL was born in Apr 1848. He died on 21 Nov 1926 in McIntosh County, Georgia. He married Susan Ann Rowe on 16 Jan 1868 in Liberty County, Georgia. She was born in Aug 1843. She died before 21 Nov 1926.

　　　　viii. WILLIAM DEAL was born about 1851 in Georgia.

Generation 4

4.　ZACHARIAH[4] DEAL (Curtis[3], Simon A.[2], John[1]) was born on 24 Feb 1838 in Telfair County, Georgia. He died on 29 Nov 1919 in Liberty County, Georgia. He married Alice Alethea Jackson, daughter of Joseph Jackson and Mary Ann Somersall on 27 Mar 1862. She was born on 27 Oct 1843 in Liberty County, Georgia. She died on 15 Aug 1915 in Darien, McIntosh County, Georgia.

More About Zachariah Deal:
Burial: Dean's Grove Cemetery, Jones, McIntosh County, Georgia
Military Service: August 27, 1861, Company H, 25Th Georgia Infantry, C.S.A.

Notes for Zachariah Deal:
Company H, 25th Georgia Infantry was known as company E then company G before becoming company H.

More About Alice Alethea Jackson:
Burial: Dean's Grove Cemetery, Jones, McIntosh County, Georgia

Zachariah Deal and Alice Alethea Jackson had the following children:
　　　　i.　JOSEPHINE[5] DEAL was born about 1864 in Georgia.

　　　　ii.　ALETHEA DEAL was born about 1868 in Georgia.

5.　JOHN WASHINGTON[4] DEAL (Curtis[3], Simon A.[2], John[1]) was born in Apr 1848. He died on 21 Nov 1926 in McIntosh County, Georgia. He married Susan Ann Rowe on 16 Jan 1868 in Liberty County, Georgia. She was born in Aug 1843. She died before 21 Nov 1926.

More About John Washington Deal:
b: Apr 1848 in Georgia
Living In: 1880 McIntosh County, Georgia
Living In: 1900 McIntosh County, Georgia
Occupation: Farmer

More About Susan Ann Rowe:
b: Aug 1843 in Georgia
Living In: 1910 McIntosh County, Georgia

John Washington Deal and Susan Ann Rowe had the following children:
　　　　JONES A.[5] DEAL was born about 1868 in Georgia.

6.　　ii. ZACHARIAH DEAL was born in Mar 1871 in Georgia. He married Eva E. Rowe, daughter of Jones Allen Rowe and Mary E. Morgan on 27 Sep 1896 in McIntosh County, Georgia. She was born on 14 Apr 1874 in Georgia. She died on 21 Apr 1928 in McIntosh County, Georgia.

　　　　iii.　ALICE DEAL was born about 1873 in Georgia.

Mary J. Deal was born about 1875 in Georgia.

Willie O. Deal was born about 1877 in Georgia.

7. vi. James Walter Deal was born in Jan 1878 in Georgia. He died on 09 Apr 1960 in McIntosh County, Georgia. He married Eva E. Rowe, daughter of Jones Allen Rowe and Mary E. Morgan on 27 Jun 1910 in McIntosh County, Georgia. She was born on 14 Apr 1874 in Georgia. She died on 21 Apr 1928 in McIntosh County, Georgia.

vii. Elliot Deal was born about 1880 in Georgia.

viii. John W. Deal was born in Jun 1881 in Georgia.

ix. Francis Deal was born in Jun 1884 in Georgia.

x. Rudolph Deal was born in Feb 1886 in Georgia.

xi. Aggie F. Deal was born in Apr 1888 in Georgia.

xii. Charley Deal was born in May 1890 in Georgia.

Generation 5

6. **Zachariah**[5] **Deal** (John Washington[4], Curtis[3], Simon A.[2], John[1]) was born in Mar 1871 in Georgia. He married Eva E. Rowe, daughter of Jones Allen Rowe and Mary E. Morgan on 27 Sep 1896 in McIntosh County, Georgia. She was born on 14 Apr 1874 in Georgia. She died on 21 Apr 1928 in McIntosh County, Georgia.

More About Zachariah Deal:
Occupation: Farmer

More About Eva E. Rowe:
Burial: 22 Apr 1928
Living In: 1910 McIntosh County, Georgia

Notes for Eva E. Rowe:
Walter Deal was listed in 1910 census as a brother in law to Eva and in the 1920 census as spouse and head of household.

Zachariah Deal and Eva E. Rowe had the following children:

Walter O.[6] Deal was born in Aug 1896 in Georgia.

Jack C. Deal was born in Feb 1900 in Georgia.

Columbus Deal was born about 1901 in Georgia.

More About Columbus Deal:
Occupation: 1920 ; Farmer, McIntosh County, Georgia

Russel Deal was born about 1905 in Georgia.

    v.   ETHEL DEAL was born about 1908 in Georgia.

    vi.   CORA DEAL was born about 1910 in Georgia.

vii   **JAMES WALTER**[5] **DEAL** (John Washington[4], Curtis[3], Simon A.[2], John[1]) was born in Jan 1878 in Georgia. He died on 09 Apr 1960 in McIntosh County, Georgia. He married Eva E. Rowe, daughter of Jones Allen Rowe and Mary E. Morgan on 27 Jun 1910 in McIntosh County, Georgia. She was born on 14 Apr 1874 in Georgia. She died on 21 Apr 1928 in McIntosh County, Georgia.

More About James Walter Deal:
Living In: 1930 McIntosh County, Georgia
Occupation: 1920; Farmer, McIntosh County, Georgia

More About Eva E. Rowe:
Burial: 22 Apr 1928
Living In: 1910 McIntosh County, Georgia

Notes for Eva E. Rowe:
Walter Deal was listed in 1910 census as a brother in law to Eva and in the 1920 census as spouse and head of household.

James Walter Deal and Eva E. Rowe had the following children:

8   i.   TULLUE[6] DEAL was born on 15 Aug 1912 in Georgia. She died on 02 Mar 2006 in Florida. She married GRIMSHAW RYALS. He was born on 25 May 1913 in Liberty County, Georgia. He died on 13 Aug 1990 in Richmond County, Georgia.

    ELIJA DEAL was born about 1917 in Georgia.

Generation 6

8.   **TULLUE**[6] **DEAL** (James Walter[5], John Washington[4], Curtis[3], Simon A.[2], John[1]) was born on 15 Aug 1912 in Georgia. She died on 02 Mar 2006 in Florida. She married **GRIMSHAW RYALS**. He was born on 25 May 1913 in Liberty County, Georgia. He died on 13 Aug 1990 in Richmond County, Georgia.

More About Tullue Deal:
Burial: Hopewell Memorial Gardens, Plant City, Hillsborough County, Florida

Notes for Tullue Deal:
Social Security death index gives a birth date of August 15, 1911.
Buried next to her son, Grimshaw.

More About Grimshaw Ryals:
Burial: Hardshell Baptist Church Cemetery, Darien, McIntosh County, Georgia
Living In: 1920 Barrington, Georgia
Living In: 1990 Blythe, Georgia
Occupation: 1913; Truck Driver
Military Service: 14 Dec 1944 ; Enlisted in U.S. Army at Fort McPherson, Georgia.

Grimshaw Ryals and Tullue Deal had the following children:

    i.   KENNETH[7] RYALS was born on 13 Apr 1937 in Savannah. Georgia. He died on 09 Apr 2008 in Brunswick, Georgia. He married BARBARA LUCILLE MUMFORD. She was born on 23 Oct 1942. She died on 01 Oct 1989 in Brunswick, Georgia. He married MARGARET HIGHSMITH.

More About Kenneth Ryals:
Burial: Brunswick Memorial Park Cemetery, Brunswick, Glynn County, Georgia
Occupation: Route salesman for Coca-Cola.
Occupation: Owned his own car detailing business

Notes for Kenneth
Ryals: Obituary
Kenneth (Kenny) G. Ryals, 70, a resident of Brunswick died Wednesday evening at his residence. Funeral Services will be 10:00 AM Saturday in the chapel of Brunswick Memorial Park Funeral Home with Rev. Wayne Manning officiating. Interment will follow in Brunswick Memorial Park Cemetery. Mr. Ryals was born in Savannah and a resident of Glynn County for 49 years and a prior resident of Cox. He had retired from Coca-Cola where he was a route salesman. He owned and operated a car detailing business. He was a wonderful husband, father and grand father, and a friend to all. He was an avid Ford owner and was a collector of Ford cars and Coca-Cola memorabilia. He is survived by his wife, Margaret Highsmith Ryals of Brunswick, two daughters, Kimberly (Kim) Waters (Todd) of Brunswick, Shirley Bedford (Mike) of Millington, TN, four step daughters, Vanessa Lee (Harry) of Hoboken, Christine Turner (Bobby) and Lynn Willis (Travis) both of Nahunta, Tina Temples (Terry) of Woodbine, one step son, Max T. Drury (Rachel) of Waverly, two sisters, Leona Simmons and Juanita Williams of Plant City, FL, two brothers, Hiram (Scooter) Ryals (Beverly) of Riverview, FL and Eugene Ryals of Plant City, FL., three grandchildren, thirteen step grandchildren, and four step great grandchildren and several nieces and nephews. He was preceded in death by his first wife, Lucille, his parents, Grimshaw and Tulla Ryals and a brother, Jimmy Ryals. Active pallbearers will be, T. J. Waters, Skippy Howard, Billy Copeland, Steve Pello, Pat Pello, Peter Santiago (Pineapple), Jay Honeycutt and Arthur Sharpe. Honorary pallbearers will be present and former employees of Brunswick Coca-Cola, Staff of third floor St. Vincent Hospital, Dr. Phillip B. Aquila and Staff, Dr. Ossi and First Coast Oncology Staff, Todd Waters, Max Drury, Dr. Robert Thompson and Staff, and Cal Thompson. Family will receive friends from 6:00-8:00 PM Friday, April 11, 2008 at Brunswick Memorial Park Funeral Home. The family request that memorial contributions be made to Hospice of the Golden Isles. Brunswick Memorial Park Funeral Home in charge of arrangements.

----

ii.   GRIMSHAW RYALS was born on 24 Mar 1944 in Savannah, Georgia. He died on 07 Mar 2004 in Plant City, Florida.

More About Grimshaw Ryals:
Burial: 10 Mar 2004 in Hopewell Memorial Gardens, Plant City, Florida

Notes for Grimshaw Ryals:
Buried next to his mother.

iii.   EVA JUANITA RYALS was born on 09 Dec 1948 in Georgia. She died on 26 Jun 2010 in Plant City, Florida. She married John Lloyd Williams about 1978.

More About Eva Juanita Ryals:
Burial: 30 Jun 2010 in Hopewell Memorial Gardens, Plant City, Florida

Notes for Eva Juanita Ryals:
Juanita "Tiny" WILLIAMS
WILLIAMS, Juanita "Tiny," 61, of Plant City, Fla., departed this life June 26, 2010. She was preceded in death by her brothers, Kenneth Ryals and Jimmy Ryals. She is survived by her husband of 32 years, John Lloyd Williams; daughter, Eva Driggs (David); grand-daughter, Amber Owens; siblings, Leona Simmons, Scooter Ryals (Bev), and Eugene Ryals; and many loving family members and friends. A celebration of life will take place at noon Wednesday, June 30, at Hopewell Funeral Home, 6005 State Road 39 S., Plant City, where the family will receive friends at 11 a.m. Interment will follow at Hopewell Memorial Gardens, Plant City. Expressions of condolence may be sent at www.hopewellfuneral.com

4. HIRAM RYALS.

5. LEONA RYALS was born on 14 Aug 1939 in Georgia. She married EDWARD WILTON SIMMONS. He was born on 29 Aug 1935 in Georgia. He died on 23 Apr 1997 in Hillsborough County, Florida. She married (2) JAMES WILLIE WELLS on 24 Apr 2011 in Plant City, Florida. He was born on 10 Aug 1936 in South Carolina. She married ALBERT J. DAVIS.

6. EUGENE RYALS was born in 1950. He married CAROL HESTER YARBROUGH. She was born in 1952.